Stalinist Realism and
Open Communism

Stalinist Realism and Open Communism

Malignant Mirror or Free Association

Ian Parker

Resistance Books

Stalinism Realism and Open Communism
Malignant Mirror or Free Association

Ian Parker

Published 2022
Resistance Books, London
info@resistancebooks.org
www.resistancebooks.org

Cover design by Adam Di Chiara

ISBN: 978-0-902869-27-1 (print)
ISBN: 978-0-902869-26-4 (e-book)

Capitalism as a global system of rule tells us that there is no alternative, and is accompanied by its terrible twin, 'stalinist realism' that works its way into ideas about political camps, bodies, identity and organisation.

Ian Parker provides an analysis and an alternative, 'open communism', which is democratic and plural, and must be built now.

Ian Parker is a revolutionary Marxist in Manchester, an activist with Anti-Capitalist Resistance, and author of *Revolutionary Keywords for a New Left* (2017: Zero Books), *Socialisms: Revolutions Betrayed, Mislaid and Unmade* (2020: Resistance Books) and *Radical Psychoanalysis and Anti-Capitalist Action* (2022: Resistance Books).

CONTENTS

CONTENTS

Introduction

Stalinist Realism

Mark Fisher gave us a cutting-edge analysis in 2009 of what he called 'capitalist realism'; the ideological claim that capitalism is the only possible reality today, that there is no alternative. Mark's analysis showed us that this kind of 'realism' locks us into place in capitalism, and is suffused with fantasies about our passivity and the impossibility of radical change. 'Realism' here is the mantra of those who want the world to stay the same, of those who want exploitation to continue as it is, of those who want to convince us to give up struggling for another world beyond capitalism.

There is an alternative, and Anti-Capitalist Resistance works alongside other revolutionary organisations here and across the world to build that alternative. Mark Fisher showed us that we need a deep analysis of the ideology of 'capitalist realism' precisely so we can better challenge it. Understanding the world, for us revolutionaries, is intimately connected to challenge and change, to struggle and transformation. That is what socialist politics is for us.

But we also face another threat, one Mark understood well, and which this little book focuses on. There is a weird flip-side of capitalist realism that pretends to offer a way out of global capitalism but which locks us all the more tightly into exploitation and oppression. That false path, a poisonous trap for the left, is 'stalinist realism' (a telling phrase we owe to comrade Ali); little s for stalinist here to mark it as a pervasive cultural-political phenomenon on the left. Stalinist realism is very present in the explicit politics of some groups that say they are communist and in the politics of their fellow travellers who are well-meaning but deeply mistaken.

Stalinist realism is a kind of weird malignant mirror of global capitalism; it repeats many of the most toxic aspects of capitalism while posing as an alternative. It is not an alternative. It is part of the problem. Here we explain what stalinist realism is, and why it needs to be avoided.

To understand what stalinist realism is, we will need to quickly backtrack to its origins, and show how it reflects and reinforces capitalism. Then we will look at different kinds of supposedly 'anti-imperialist' and 'feminist' arguments made by stalinist realist politics, arguments that seem to be progressive but are in fact deeply reactionary, betraying anti-imperialist and feminist struggles.

These arguments have consequences for organisation and struggle. Revolutionary democracy is, against the stalinist realist tradition, the basis for authentic anti-capitalist resistance. That is the basis of a real alternative, open communism.

Open communism

There are plenty of corrupt pretenders to 'communism' that have smeared the word and turned it into exactly the kind of bureaucratic police state that the right-wing defenders of capitalism always said it would be. And capitalism benefits from this weird mirror image of capitalist un-freedom; the existence of authoritarian closed states that proclaim that they are communist or those regimes that are ruled by 'communist' parties effectively frightens people off from demanding an alternative, from building an alternative for themselves.

We need to open the roads to communism, open communism. We want a world that is just and fair, and where we hold the earth and what we produce in common as a shared resource for all. Almost everything we are told about communism is what we do not want; ranging from the idea that it is about state control to the claim that the ruling party will take away your toothbrush.

We are wary about setting out blueprints for exactly what a communist society will look like. Apart from the time taken piddling about tinkering with this or that rule for setting up a new society in a completely abstract way – an activity for nitpickers that turns communism from a practical accomplishment into some kind of 'idea' in the clouds – any blueprint drawn up now will simply reflect present-day life and limitations of living under capitalism now.

We do not know how things will unfold, from where, and when, and that means 'communism' is much more about a process than an endpoint. And, let's face it, with the climate crisis condemning the globe to a fiery hell, it is possible we will not get to that endpoint at all. What counts is what we do now, how we struggle and what we build.

That's why we show in this little book why freedom is essential to communism, and that includes the kinds of limited freedom that were stolen from us when capitalism was developed as a political-economic system, developed on the basis of the enclosure of land and control of our creative abilities. That freedom entails opening up to an international dimension of struggle, connecting with the struggles of all of the oppressed and valuing plurality of struggles, plurality of perspectives.

Against closed bureaucratic fake-communism

– the heritage of tragic failed revolutions and counterrevolutions – we open communism to a transition that anticipates the forms of life we want in the forms of struggle we engage in now. We should not – as some of the hard-faced 'old left' imagine we should – do bad things now as means to the supposed good ends. That is a bankrupt dead-end. Instead, we realise our visions of communism now in the very process of making the transition. Making small significant steps is not the opposite of revolution, but the prerequisite for it as we open communism now.

2

Stalinism

Stalinism is one form of defeat and demoralisation, of failure of revolutionary hopes, and it has a brutal practical existence, a kind of 'reality', in the bureaucratic hierarchical regimes that appeared in different parts of the world after the 1917 Russian revolution. That revolution, the 1917 'October' revolution, was a popular uprising, a time of revolutionary democracy both inside the Bolshevik Party, Russia's communist party, and in the wider society. It was an opportunity and moment for radical experimentation, a flowering of rebellious movements in the fields of politics and art, of national liberation and sexual politics.

That revolution was crushed by the intervention of the surrounding capitalist countries, by capitalist regimes intent on preventing the revolution from spreading, preventing it connecting with rebellions in other parts of Europe, other parts of the world. It was crushed in part by those interventions and by the civil war that led to the militarisation of Russian society as it tried to defend itself. But it was also crushed by the internal counterrevolution that rose on the back of that militarisation.

During the 1920s Joseph Stalin came to power in the new Soviet Union, and the 'soviets', which were once the basis of revolutionary democracy, were turned into tools of control. In place of open debate there was the implementation of a line from the top, from the Kremlin in Moscow, and Stalin ruled from the height of a bureaucratic apparatus that betrayed the revolution. The communist party directed by Stalin claimed to defend the revolution, but it betrayed it, and the 'Stalinist' Soviet Union became a kind of mirror-image of the worst, most oppressive capitalist regimes.

Democracy

Capitalist regimes hypocritically complained about the lack of democracy in the Soviet Union, but loved that Stalinism was smearing the reputation of revolutionary socialist politics in blood. Capitalism, and the kind of 'capitalist realism' that tells you that there is no alternative, was mirrored by Stalinism and a 'stalinist realism' that tells you that the only alternative is oppressive and controlling. This is how stalinist realism appears in the politics of the communist parties around the world loyal to Stalin, a kind of realism that tells you there is no hope for socialism except as a kind of military discipline.

Revolutionary movements had to defy Stalinism to overthrow capitalism in their own countries. As an ideological force stalinist realism insisted that the only reality was either capitalism or bureaucratic control, that these two systems should peacefully coexist, and not interfere with the functioning of each 'camp' or part of the world. If you took sides, you were told, it is one side or the other, either with capitalism or with the bureaucracy, and so with Stalinism.

China broke from Stalin, but after its own revolution against capitalism it quickly adopted the same kind of political form in which the local communist party had been schooled in, part of the oppressive mirror-world of stalinist realism.

That Stalinist mirror-world gathered many fellow-travellers to support the bureaucratic regimes, useful idiots willing to overlook abuses of power, cover up for the crimes of the regimes they were loyal to. And so when they argued for 'peace' and 'peaceful coexistence', for example, it was only to reinforce the idea that there were two ways of living, capitalist or 'socialist', and that the 'socialist' parts of the world were a heaven where man did not exploit man.

The joke made by revolutionaries was that in the Stalinist countries that claimed to be 'socialist', it was not so different; under capitalism man exploited man, but in the Soviet Union, it was the other way round. And with that exploitation came the reinforcement of other kinds of oppression, including the revival of the nuclear family and the power of men over women, as well as colonialism, with Great Russian chauvinism rearing its head again to control the less powerful nations in its assumed domain.

Reform

Attempts to 'reform' the Soviet Union, and attempts to bring about a 'cultural revolution' and then implement 'socialism with Chinese characteristics' in Beijing, showed that there was always desire for something better. People in those countries who had been told by the regimes that this is 'socialism' demanded that the regimes were true to their word, and attempted to implement socialist politics for themselves, by themselves. Those movements were beaten back time and again, and the bureaucratic regimes eventually transformed from a brutal mirror-image of the capitalist world into a part of it, becoming fully capitalist.

Sometimes, as in China, the old 'socialist' rhetoric was used, is still used, to justify repression, but Russia and China today are capitalist, tied into global capitalism, part of the chains of colonial and imperialist expansion, and signed up to the forms of racial and sexual oppression that makes power under capitalism work so efficiently. The 'stalinist realism' of the old regimes, and their supporters in communist parties around the world, had to adapt to the new reality, to the globalisation of capitalism that has become the only 'realistic' option, with no alternative whatsoever.

After the final incorporation of Russia and China and its various dependent satellite regimes in Eastern Europe and South East Asia, is the world of 'capitalist realism'. And in such a world it really does seem that if you are to be 'realistic', you must accept that capitalism is the only game in town. You have to play by its rules, give up hope for a better world, for socialism. But there is a twist, and the twist is that Stalinism is not dead.

The old military-style bureaucratic conception of 'socialist' politics still lives, and while it pretends to be an ally of the left, it is a deadly enemy of it, kicking us while we are down. Stalinist realism is the kind of politics that tells you that if you dislike capitalism, if you are searching for another reality, then this, obedient and stupid agreement with bureaucratic power, is the only alternative you can hope for.

3

Camps

It is an overwhelming problem that there was always a material basis for capitalist realism – systems of production and consumption that locked people in place as if there was no alternative – and for stalinist realism in the ruling ideology of the actually-existing bureaucratic regimes that claimed to be socialist. There still is that material basis for both, for global capitalism and its malignant mirror-politics. The material basis for stalinist realism today is the existence of the regimes that are now capitalist but still hypocritically use old socialist symbolism to cloak their agendas, and the existence of the old communist parties that are still geared to the needs of those regimes.

The two main power-bases for stalinist realism today are Vladimir Putin's Russia and Xi Jinping's China, and stalinist realism is the ideological force that glues some well-meaning radicals into the agenda of those regimes. The material apparatus of the regimes extends into the so-called 'communist' parties that cover up the crimes of Putin and Jinping, and into the network of 'front' organisations controlled by those parties, as well as the array of different movements that buy into stalinist realism.

There are those who mistakenly believe that China is 'socialist', and there are even those pretending that Russia has not fully embraced capitalism. These lines are handed down by the leaderships of the 'communist' parties, even though many of the members of those parties do not really buy that. The pity is that there are groups on the left who know well that these are capitalist countries, but their own ways of organising fits with the way those regimes operate, and they simply overlook what their own analysis shows them for pragmatic political purposes.

Stalinist realism as a bureaucratic top-down way of doing politics – a parody of alienated capitalist ideology and betrayal of revolutionary politics – has a number of components. One powerful component is the claim that the world is divided into different 'camps' and that you need to make a choice, that if you want to oppose capitalism and its own militarised NATO world then you must, of necessity, opt for the other camp, as if that is a progressive alternative. The illusion that there is a 'progressive camp' in the world now is an integral part of stalinist realism.

Strength

The trap is that strong state power presents itself as the only alternative to apparently looser liberal free-capitalism. So it seems as if when you oppose capitalism you have to opt for one of the strong states, and sign up to the kind of command politics that one of the old 'communist' parties engages in. At its worst, that means being obedient, following the rules of a kind of 'democratic centralism' that is highly centralised, and staying silent about abuses of power. Internal democracy is viewed as a threat by some left groups, and this leads them into campism when they should know better.

By forcing a choice between support for capitalist powers or one of the old 'socialist' states, global politics is reduced to a zero-sum game, which was always one of the ideological pillars of the Cold War when Stalinism was in full force. Forcing a choice for one camp or the other, as if Moscow or Beijing were somehow more progressive than Washington or London, is 'campism'. Campism as part of the ideological worldview of stalinist realism then subjects you to the host of explicit and implicit conspiratorial propaganda ploys promoted by naïve supporters and algorithm-driven internet bots.

This is where you are made to draw lines. For example, lines between the supposedly progressive and 'socialist' regime in Beijing attempting to bring 'civilization' to its eastern regions, and to the Uighur Muslims in Xinxiang concentration camps. They are not really 'camps', you say, it is a fiction, invented by the West. Then, perhaps, you

take the next step, and start to disbelieve Tibetans
who are suffering under the military occupation
because they are in the wrong 'camp', the Western camp. That is stalinist realism, as if the only
possible alternative to the rotten West are these
supposedly nicer regimes.

Because you oppose 'Western intervention',
you then make the fatal mistake of believing the
propaganda of, say, the Assad regime in Syria, that
tells you that the main threat is Islamic terrorist
insurgents who are being bravely opposed by the
friendly Russian air-strikes. Or you proclaim that
'the main enemy is at home', which is true, but
which then leads you to forget the deadly enemies
of those you should be in solidarity with, the main
enemy in their homes. In short, you risk ending up
in the crazy mirror-world of stalinist realism, even
painting the White Helmet humanitarian support
initiatives as imperialist puppets because they are
critical of the Assad regime, or even denying that
this regime carried out deadly gas attacks.

Because NATO is a Western imperialist alliance
– which it is, no doubt, and we should call for it
to be dismantled as one of our tasks – then you

slide into the campist assumption that those who are opposing NATO are the good guys. There is a real danger that you slide into a pacifist refusal to send people arms to defend themselves, abstain on supporting struggles for liberation. Then, bit by bit, you are drawn into the conspiracy theories promoted by the Kremlin, the idea that Ukraine is a Western puppet regime, that Ukraine's attempt to assert its independence is merely a ploy to provoke Putin, who only has Russia's legitimate 'security concerns' in mind. Does he hell; his concerns are for his own security and property.

Sides

The pity is that stalinist realism sucks in revolutionaries who once proudly declared that they refused to take sides, that they would choose neither Washington nor Moscow but struggle for international socialism. They were right then, and were suspicious of Stalinism to the point where they would never side with a brutal regime or cover up happening there. They were right then in the face of sustained propaganda from the West, when it was more difficult to get information out from inside Russia and China about what was really happening.

Now, with almost immediate online contact with our comrades around the world, we are, paradoxically, faced with more complete ideological control, the world of 'capitalist realism' where it seems as if the only possible global reality is international capitalism. And, as its mirror image, we have stalinist realism and its ideological apparatuses pumping out the message that we must choose, between our own government or theirs, between Washington or Moscow, or Beijing.

As with capitalist realism, this suffuses power with fantasy. Here the fantasy is that we can escape from a world of 'soft power', a world of empty alienating consumer fake choice, a world in which we are free to shop but not to collectively organise our own lives for the good of all. The fantasy that stalinist realism provokes and feeds is that there is good power, state power you can happily offer yourself to, that you can trust what those leaders tell you, and that deaths in Xinxiang or Tibet or Syria or Ukraine are myths or a price worth paying.

Those deaths at the hands of Putin or Jinping, you tell yourself, are not deaths at all – they are fabricated, made up, untrue – or they are little deaths compared to the bigger world picture in which our imperialism and its NATO weapons is finally being opposed and could be ended by regimes that are fantastically and marvellously stronger. Our weakness, our helplessness, finally finds a force that is more powerful, that will rescue us, so it is best to be grateful, keep quiet about the problems, and choose the good camp.

4

Bodies

Stalinist realism loves strong borders, strong boundaries, it loves to know what is what and who fits where. And so it is not surprising that, just as Stalin revived the idea of the nuclear family inside the Soviet Union to make the regime rest on millions of little points of power – little dictatorships in every home – so 'family' and 'normal' family relationships are an obsession of Putin and Jinping.

While revolutionary Marxists seek alliances with all the movements of the oppressed, of Lesbian and Gay, Queer and Transgender movements as part of their fight for a world in which we are free to be who we want to be, stalinist realism tells you what reality you must accept and live with, what you cannot even think about changing. LGBTQI+ groups have been closed down in China now because they pose a threat to the regime. That is not only because those groups were places to speak that escaped the immediate control of the regime, but because sexual freedom and experimentation itself throws the regime into question. A key feature of stalinist realism is that there should be state control of bodies, that our bodies ourselves are not for us to experience and define and live in.

In Russia, the legal prohibition on what Putin calls 'pretended family relationships' – that is, gay and lesbian sexuality – is accompanied by state violence, persecution and imprisonment and by para-state physical attacks by religious and quasi-fascist groups. This situation inside Russia, and in China, mirrors the worst of the homophobic attacks on the gay and lesbian communities in the West. Control of bodies is a key feature of stalinist realism, and ideological control is enforced through fake-scientific knowledge about what 'normal' and 'abnormal' sexual and gender development is.

Trans

Stalinist realism makes deep claims about the nature of reality, and especially the supposed reality
of the essential biological difference between kinds
of bodies. It defines 'reality', not only at the level
of experience – of who and how we love and what
kind of beings we imagine ourselves to be – but
also at the level of biological difference. Just as
stalinist realism wants to define who is a Russian
and to deny the ethnic reality of Ukrainians – they
are told they do not exist, and Putin blames Lenin,
among others, for promoting Ukrainian independence – so this kind of 'realism' pretends to define
who is Chinese and depict Tibetans as relics of
the past, and Muslims in Xinxiang as uncivilised
remnants.

As with nations and strong borders beloved by
old Stalinist states – something those states learnt
from Western colonialism and imperialism, something that mirrors capitalist realism and the brutal
control of populations – so it is with sexed bodies,
and the division of people in the world into 'real'

men and 'real' women. Those who travel across borders and claim their identity are treated as a threat, bodies to be contained, and those who travel across traditional gender categories are likewise treated as a threat, to be medically treated, corrected.

This is why there is such hostility among the stalinist realists and their fellow-travellers today to trans people, to those who either want to transition from their assigned gender to another or are 'non-binary', that is, refuse to conform to existing gender categories that enforce masculine and feminine stereotypes about how men and women should behave and think. Trans people are a threat to stalinist realism, and here is a paradox that pits stalinist realism against capitalist realism.

Order

Capitalist realism is organised around the fiction of free choice, and makes it seem like you can consume what you like so long as you have the ability to pay for it – you need money to survive, and for that you need to sell your labour power. There-fore, Western capitalism is ready to incorporate different gender and sexual lifestyles, to 'pink-wash' exploitation to make it seem freer. There is for sure plenty of homophobia and transphobia under capitalism – suspicion and hatred of lives that are different, that do not fit – but the ideological watchwords of neoliberal capitalism are freedom, flexibility and choice.

These watchwords are fictions, and they obscure the lives of trans people, just as they do of lesbian and gay people, even at the same time as they pretend to 'include' them and make them more visible as market-niche consumers. This is part of the structure of capitalist realism; it seems as if everything is free and open, and as if anyone who complains has a personal problem, a grudge; neoliberalism strips away state support while increasing police powers, and it puts the onus on the individual to struggle to define themselves against a hostile world and hostile laws.

What stalinist realism offers is certainty, law and order. In place of the apparent anarchy of the market-place in the West, in the capitalist heartlands of imperialism, where people are made to fend for themselves and their families, the supposedly 'post-socialist' states, with Russia and China as the core examples, offer security and control. With security, being told who you are, including whether you are really a man or a woman, comes control, where the state will pathologise you if you step out of line, if you step out of your assigned sexuality or gender.

Stalinist realism thrives on order, and it promises – at the level of its direct political intervention in the lives of LGBTQI+ people and at the level of fantasy for everyone anxious about who they are and what they should do – an ordered world. The watchwords of stalinist realism are boundaries, borders and an ordered world. This order divides the world into 'camps', spheres of influence, and it divides populations into men and women who should healthily and happily fit themselves into the bodies described by the Stalinist realist 'scientists'.

Stalinist realism is a political practice and fantasy of order – things in their place, people in their national territories governed by strong states, and bodies that have the right kind of desires for other kinds of bodies – and so it is, among other things, a form of organisation, and organisation of our desire to change this world. Actually, it is a form of organisation that blocks change.

5

Identity

We desire to change the world. We know things are wrong, and that this capitalist world is not all there is. It came into being at a particular historical point, has not lasted that long, and it can be replaced. There is an alternative. But that desire is continually thwarted and distorted, and we have been betrayed time and again. It is understandable that, with the disappearance of the so-called 'socialist bloc' – the Soviet Union as a monolithic closed other world and China as an ideologically-rigid Maoist version of Stalinism – capitalist realism takes hold. Then it really does seem as if there is no alternative.

It is in that context that the fantasy that there must be something beyond capitalism becomes so alluring – and it is good that there is always that hope – but it is tragic that it becomes attached to actually-existing powerful apparatuses, whether of nation states or the organisations that promote them and tell us that things are really better there. We know that things are not better there.

The Internet gives us bewildering, competing images of the world and contradictory information about what is happening across the globe, but it also gives us quicker, more immediate access to the struggles of the exploited and oppressed inside Russia and China. And so, the desire for change runs up against reality, and it is in the grip of stalinist realism that reality itself gives way to fantasy, to the desperate fantastic hope that things must be different, must change, that someone else has done it, and can do it for us.

Fantasy

Stalinist realism rests on peculiar and toxic ideological mutations of our all-too human hope and fantasy that another world is possible, and it anchors that fantasy onto capitalist states and state agendas that are a malignant mirror-image of global capitalism, not at all the alternatives they pretend to be. It fixes our desire for change on things – leaders, states, parties, symbols – that seem to be eternal, ordered, never-changing, and that is one of the attractions in a capitalist world characterised by mind-spinning change, uncertainty and precarious anxiety about what will come next.

Identity is one of the underlying motifs of stalinist realism, the sense that things can be fixed in place, and that we ourselves can be secure in knowing where and what we are. Some nationalist and transphobe versions of this concern with borders and boundaries pretends to tell us about what is common to all humankind while betraying that promise. Instead of bringing us together, each respecting what is different about the others, making that diversity of experience and politics our strength, we are separated into our different identities. We are separated from each other, but it is not the 'identity' of the oppressed that is the problem.

One of the longstanding political lines rolled out in the peace and anti-racist movements by supporters of the various 'communist' parties loyal to Moscow, for example, was that racism as such is divisive, and that there are no 'real' racial differences between human beings. Racism was here countered by the well-meaning slogan 'one race the human race'. That line reflected the material interests of the Stalinist bureaucracies in their attempts to govern many different populations, whether in the Soviet Union or in China, and while local folk communities were patronised it was only to better rule them, to make them good citizens, loyal to the centrally-organised state apparatus.

There is truth in the claim that there is one human race, but this truth has to be built, fought for, and it can only be fought for effectively, and with respect accorded to those who have suffered from racism, if we do take seriously how capitalism, and Stalinism, profited from division, from segregation.

The fantasy here, and it is not only a reactionary fantasy – it is an understandable response and challenge to racism – is that we are all the same, that there is something universal in our collective struggle as we work together to overthrow capitalism and build a better world, build socialism. The danger – and here the fantasy is not so progressive – is that as people are rendered the same, the 'otherness' of the different lives of human beings is wiped away, and we end up with a fiction. The fiction is that the people of a community or a nation or a world are 'homogeneous', all the same and with obvious common interests.

Walls

Then the desire for the working class to be the universal class is turned into a fetish, something we become attached to, and make a short circuit to arrive at it; we make an ideological short circuit that along the way leads us to trivialise or ignore what structural power differences among human beings under capitalism do to our different experiences of exploitation and oppression, of what it is to be a human being. Then, and this is where a peculiar and dangerous twist on the fantasy that we must all be the same has disastrous political effects, even the claim that there is racism is seen as 'divisive'.

This is where the peculiar stalinist realist obsession with the supposed threat of 'identity' comes into play. This takes different forms, including in some places the fantasy that the working class is a kind of 'red wall' disturbed and disrupted by the enemy of 'identity politics'. That fantasy of the working class as a 'red wall' is a fantasy that there is an already united non-racist homogeneous working class just waiting for the correct leadership by the right party, and that this working class has been somehow hurt and 'left behind' by the identity-politics promoted by anti-racist and LGBTQI+ movements.

In other words, instead of racism and sexism and other forms of oppression being seen as divisive forces, enabling the ruling class to divide and rule us, the attempts to name and call out racism and so on, are themselves treated as threats, as forms of division. The 'unity' of the working class is then used against the oppressed, and even sometimes used to defend the 'unity' of a colonial power against nations asserting their rights.

We need to face the fact that the lives of people under global capitalism are contradictory, diverse, complicated, and that we carry into our revolutionary organisations all of the toxic stuff – racism, sexism, assumptions about ability and disability – that capitalism brings into the world and makes use of and reinforces. Claims to identity empower the oppressed, and enable them to argue for their rights inside and outside of left organisations; they are not a threat.

We need to face the challenge inside our revolutionary organisations as well as in the outside world – in communities, trades unions and political parties – of taking seriously structural racism and sexism. We cannot assume that we are homogeneous, all the same. We are different, and with that difference there is potentially greater combined power for change.

6

Organisation

At the heart of revolutionary Marxism as a theory and anti-capitalist resistance as a practice is a radical conception of organisation, of how we organise ourselves and how we might organise the world. That radical conception of organisation was effectively present in the flowering of alternative ways of living during the revolutions and liberation struggles that formed the Soviet Union, the Chinese state and independent nations that were formed as they broke from colonial control.

That radical conception of organisation has been transformed and refined by the encounter of revolutionary Marxists with feminists, anti-racist and de-colonial activists as well as with radical disability activists who showed us how capitalism relies on certain limited forms of 'normality' and able-bodied selves, the kinds of selves that capitalism can buy labour power from and sell its goods to.

The tragedy of the revolutions betrayed is that, among other things, structured top-down organisation becomes a fetish, and in place of authentic revolutionary democracy we have centralised command and control. In that way, one of the key aspects of stalinist realism is embedded in left organisations, and the world is organised around leaders and followers, a supposedly fully conscious 'vanguard'. The ordinary members and fellow-travellers are then treated as a kind of part-time chorus, kept in the dark most of the time, and keeping themselves in the dark so they don't have to think about what is being done in the 'camps' they have been supporting and endorsing.

Centralisation

In place of a genuine democratic collectivisation of experience – the bringing together of diverse perspectives and struggles – stalinist realism relies on the direct centralisation of politics. This is also the case in the so-called 'democratic centralist' organisations that claim to have broken from Stalinism and who should know better. In this way, stalinist realism replicates itself in the many little sects run by little tin-pot leaders.

Members and followers are expected to give their lives to the group, and anxiety is induced in them; they become anxious that their political worlds will disintegrate if the group collapses and the prospect of political change will be destroyed. This is where fantasy in stalinist realism once again plays a crucial role alongside pragmatic political manoeuvring. At the same time as members of parties are expected to 'hold the line' in public, not be open about the internal debates, they begin to live that divided and secretive experience inside themselves. They forget what they really think, and their own doubts are pushed aside, 'repressed'.

Then, instead of delegates who are accountable

and can be quickly and easily recalled, replaced if necessary, organisations and movements are composed of 'representatives' who are expected to fall into line with the demands of the leadership bodies. This is the world of the party or campaign congress where resolutions are fait accompli and, finally, when simply asked if 'anyone is against', we see who is against, who will be suspected of creating divisions or 'factional' disputes.

This mode of operation is replicated also in many supposedly 'non-Stalinist' or 'anti-Stalinist' groups that specialise in their own control-freak political operations. In the process, and as a key part of the stalinist realist worldview, members are inducted into a paranoiac way of dealing with 'outsiders' who, if they cannot be recruited, are treated as suspect, even sometimes with accusations made that anyone who disagrees must in be either a direct police agent or perhaps, in an insidiously irrefutable claim, an 'unwitting' police agent.

In some contexts, trades unions are treated as relay points, 'fronts' for the political organisation instead of the autonomous self-organised expression of working class consciousness and resistance.

That may either take the form of a direct obvious connection between a trade union and a political party, or as an indirect more covert smearing of political opponents and control of the apparatus, with those who raise political differences accused of introducing political divisions. One of the hallmarks of stalinist realism is the closing of political debate around a set agenda and the accusation levelled against anyone who disagrees that they are creating a diversion or distraction, perhaps at the behest of outside forces.

Fronts

Stalinist realism is organisationally structured around parties and leaders who know what's what – in the old days it was Joseph Stalin himself or Chairman Mao who ruled the roost – and by a range of different organisations and movements that are gently 'guided', sometimes directly controlled by those in the know and at the centre of things.

Stalinist realist fronts usually work in a way

that is closely connected with national and sometimes 'red-brown' nationalist agendas. That is, a
favourite kind of stalinist realist front is a 'popular'
alliance of close and distant individuals and groups
– those that can be directly trusted and organised
and those who are willing to follow along – around
a limited range of issues, with other political differences and debates pushed into the background.
Those who raise questions about stitch-ups in
choice of representatives or political lines are then
marginalised or slandered as 'splitters'.

A special case of this kind of popular front
is in the liberation movements in the so-called
'developing world' where the Stalinist states were
historically able to trade their industrial and military power with 'liberation' movements and then
emerging nation states. Here again, a command
and control bureaucratic model of leadership is enforced, with local leaders who resist risking being
sidelined or even murdered.

Today under the fullest spread of stalinist realism among left groups, locally and globally, it is the
technical expertise and commercial and financial
power of the Chinese and Russian states – through

the 'belt and road' initiative or control of gas-supply lines – that underpins this colonial control. Now stalinist realism becomes part of the ideological apparatus of imperialism in the networks that promise to provide an alternative to 'Western' civilisation – seen as the bad camp – but which still lock dependent nations and political leaderships into real and symbolic debt traps.

This is where the malignant mirror-world of stalinist realism locks us all the more tightly into global capitalism. It is often said by the right that there is no alternative but this. Stalinist realism repeats the mantra of capitalist realism, that there is no alternative. But there is. Open communism.

7

Freedom

Open communism is more than simply saying that another world is possible. There is something in the claim to communism that transcends our miserable everyday reality, and that is driven by the kind of impulse Karl Marx described when he was writing about the limits of religion. Spiritual yearning, a desire for something beyond capitalism, is not something communists should squash but that they should welcome.

Marx tells us that religion is 'the sigh of an oppressed creature', that it is 'the heart of a heartless world'. Our hopes and desires in our sighing hearts are distorted by organised religion, but communism opens the way for those desires to be realised in the real world. Some academic philosophers will say that communism is an 'idea', and that it exists as a timeless state of being that we can then find a way to put into practice. But it is more than that.

Religion

Communism is not a form of religion, not a magical idealist blueprint, and not something already in our heads that needs to be made real. It is more than that, going beyond the limited frame of paradise that is promised by religious leaders. Here is a paradox, for we are suspicious of the big promises of future paradise on earth or heaven and so we promise less, but in the process we open up the possibilities for far more. Questioning what we are told about the way the world is – and following Marx's own favourite dictum to 'doubt everything' – we realise the best of spiritual hopes but ground them in reality.

We can share ideas about what communism

might involve based on what we resist, based on what we refuse in this wretched reality that puts a price on everything, that turns everything into a 'commodity', a thing to be bought and sold. But, in the process, we need to practically build it now.

Communism is not a promise that your suffering here will be redeemed in some distant future, and in that sense it is the opposite of religious systems that merely offer consolation and tell you to accept things as they are now. We resist, and on the basis of our resistance we go beyond the closed confined hopes of individuals and their prayers to a higher being to resolve their pain, and we ground our resistance in collective struggle.

So, communism is not an 'idea' into which we pour our fantasies and wait, not 'abstract' as a kind of ideal model or blueprint in our heads, but something we will need to piece together, as a collective practice. Communism needs to be grounded in what we can do now so that we are building it on real-world foundations, doing that so we can really make it possible.

Practice

It is possible, and we know that because there are already real-world practical foundations for it. Take, for example, the existence of money as a universal equivalent for all other goods, all of the other things we create and consume. Capitalism has created this strange commodity – money as a thing to be bought and sold – at the very same time as it turns human beings into commodities, into things that are bought and sold. Our labour and our bodies are turned into things.

This strange substance, money under capitalism, is, we Marxists say, 'dialectical'; that is, it is contradictory and, under pressure, mutates into its opposite. Dialectically-speaking, money is both a trap and an opportunity. The tragedy is that, even for the super-rich – and we don't feel sorry for them – it is a trap, it does not bring happiness. We consume things that we are told will make us happy, but they do not, and as we pay we try, in some strange way, to wish away the fact that we are just exchanging one commodity, money, for something else, the commodity we are buying. Then it is a trap.

But money enables things to happen, not when it is hoarded in banks but when it is put to work in building progressive alternatives to profit-driven capitalism. While capitalism is driven by the search for profit, destroying people's lives and the planet through 'capital accumulation', we together in our social movements share and use money in a different way, and as we circulate money in solidarity with people close to us and far away from us we participate in something universal. Then money is an opportunity.

What is crucial here, and this is what makes this potentially part of the movement toward open communism, is that this use of money is more transparent and the systems that put it to work are democratically accountable. Every little left group and campaign knows this and goes in this direction with fund-raising and the collection of membership dues from members, and what marks out that use of money from being a mind-numbing commodity is that it is collective. It really then becomes the basis for something universal.

Yes, maybe we'll do without money under communism, and it is often said that the communists will one day 'abolish' money. That doesn't mean that they'll burn your banknotes or melt your credit cards or siphon off the cryptocurrency now. What it means is that in the practical movement toward communism we will turn this money hoarded by a few very rich people into a resource that we put to work for all of us. Then, eventually, we will be able to do without it.

Communism is a 'dialectical' movement that transforms reality because it takes reality seriously, takes seriously the structure of reality under capitalism and the obstacles thrown in our way – obstacles that include the organisation of military coups by the capitalist state and lurid propaganda about what the 'communists' will do if they seize power. As part of that dialectical movement grounded in material reality, 'dialectical materialism', money will be transformed from being in the world of Mammon – the demon god of greed – into a tool of change, a materialisation of collective action.

8

Commons

Communism means seizing back what was once ours. Once upon a time we shared the land, hunting and gathering, making use of natural resources. True, that use of the land began a process of plunder and exploitation, as if the environment and the other animal species we share the planet with are only there to be subject to the needs of human beings.

That is a process scientists now agree set in place what they call the 'Anthropocene' epoch, something that took final catastrophic form with the rise of industrial capitalism. Perhaps we ecosocialist Marxists might better name this epoch the

'Capitalocene' since it is capital accumulation and the rapacious search for profit that drives the destruction of our ecology now.

Capitalism was only possible with the brutal enclosure of our common land, of the 'commons' as what we together inhabited and made use of. Enclosure is the diametric opposite of communism. Communism is the seizing back of the commons, enabling us to be aware of nature and other animal species not as a mere 'environment' external to us, but an ecology that we are an intimate part of. Capitalism requires enclosure and separation, 'environment', while communism enables sharing and connection, ecology.

Enclosure

Enclosure of the land separated what we lived on into walled-off private property, and so we were forced off our shared land, and made to buy it back or rent it in little portions fit for individuals and their families to survive in while they equipped themselves to work, work for others.

This enclosure and rent is theft, repeated insulting theft of what we could together make use of.

That violent theft of what once belonged to us all is perpetuated in the private ownership of huge tracts of land, some of which is generously leased back by landowners or enclosed by the capitalist state, a state dedicated to the interests of those with property or those who treat those they employ as their property.

Enclosure of land is thus, as capitalism develops and spreads around the world, closely followed by enclosure of bodies. This happens through colonial expeditions from the developing industrial centres of capitalism – the 'West' – that are concerned with harvesting natural resources and turning local people into things to be bought and sold. The slave trade and the racist history of enclosure is at the heart of capitalism, not a mere unfortunate add on. That is why decolonisation is at the heart of communism as the seizing back of the planet by all of us as internationalists.

Cooperation

Communism pits cooperation, conscious collective activity, against enclosure as the mindless control of individuals divided from each other by others as they accumulate capital. The commons, the material basis of communism, were enclosed, but it is important to know that they are still here. There is still much of the commons that has not been completely enclosed, and the history of capitalism is also a history of the struggle of colonised and working people for the commons.

That struggle has conserved key elements of the commons and has partially succeeded in seizing back the commons. The commons as the material practical basis for communism has been fought for, and now we need to fight for all of it, for open communism.

Here it is around us, limited, imperfect, not always democratically organised, but a collective accomplishment that we need to defend. It is here in the medical and welfare support we have demanded through our collective struggle, here in hard-won state provision, for example, as a 'spirit' of the strength of the labour movement.

It is even there in the millions of contributions, financial and practical to charity. Yes, charity as the benevolent giving of things to the poor soothes and covers over the exploitation that produces poverty in the first place – charity is perfume in the sewers of capitalism – but the impulse to care for others, the desire to respond to distress and to do that through organisations dedicated to support and sometimes to solidarity, is also an expression of something of the commons, of what we have in common as human beings.

The commons are present in the trade unions as the defence of rights and safety at work through agreements fought for in bitter struggle with employers. In each case, when the commons have not been directly enclosed and privatised, what is 'communist' about them is distorted, closed, bureaucratised. We see this when unions repeat structures of obedience, or, a little example of patriarchal micro-aggression, tell their representatives, including women, to dress up nicely to speak to employers. Then, as part of our work in and alongside unions we need to open things up as part of anti-capitalist struggle.

The taking of the commons – through enclosure and privatisation – and the exploitation of our labour power as private ownership for a period of time each day, did not at all mean that capitalism replaced an earlier paradise of complete shared ownership. If there was once some kind of 'communal' life before capitalism it was a life of scarcity and violence, of conflict and control, including patriarchal control of women's bodies by men.

Some look back to a pre-historical time of 'early' or 'primitive' matriarchal communism, but we cannot ever know if this romantic picture is true. It does give us hope that things could be different from the way things are now, but what is for sure is that communism built on the basis of plenty – plenty of what is good for us and good for all on the basis of our creative ability to produce enough for everyone – will be very different from the world before capitalism.

Capitalism is not always all bad; Marx, for example, saw it as a once progressive force and as globalising in the best sense of the term, enabling connections between people and the internationalism that today infuses our politics as revolutionary

Marxists. The dramatic increase in innovation and technology is something we can and must make use of.

Communists do not wipe away the past, start from year zero, but conserve and build on what human beings have been able to achieve so far. So, our communism is not a return to a closed limited pre-industrial world, but values the growth of care and creativity over the drive for economic growth and profit. Ours is open communism.

9

Intersections

Open communism is open to new and unexpected connections between people, and with the world, with the ecology of the planet and the species we share the planet with. Open communism is ecosocialist and feminist and anti-racist, attentive to the different ways we unthinkingly treat others as separate and lesser than us, the way we 'disable' others.

We listen and respond to demands, and we have had to do that to turn the limited, closed and sometimes authoritarian forms of party and state control that claimed to be socialist into something more genuinely communist, internationalist and 'intersectional'. That has involved, and will continue to involve, contradiction and moments of hesitation, uncertainty and puzzling about how to keep things open, how to open things up more.

The path to open communism is not a smooth easy path, but is as much about working with conflict among ourselves as it is engaging in productive conflict with those who are determined to hold onto their privilege and power.

Internationalism

With globalisation – the malign colonial harvesting of natural resources and bodies and the spread of capitalism as a political-economic system around the world – there always was a progressive potential for connection between peoples, a positive open globalisation of resistance and solidarity. That is the material basis of the spirit of internationalist struggle and organisation. And with that, as a necessary part of internationalism, a linking of struggles against global capitalism and its imperialist endeavours to subject one kind of peoples to another with struggles against racism.

That 'intersection' of struggles is part of open communism. It is a genuine alternative to the attempt to turn anti-colonial movements into pawns in a power-game between blocs, between a capitalist camp and a supposedly anti-imperialist or progressive camp, still worse the attempt to turn leaders of anti-colonial or anti-imperialist movements into ventriloquist puppets of closed militarised bureaucracies.

The working class is a 'universal' class in the sense of it being the source and materialisation of the labour power that underpins, makes possible, capitalism as a global system. This material class basis of internationalism is different from the particular 'identity' of the ruling class in one of the imperialist nations devoted to sucking in resources from other places for its own enrichment. And this is different from the nascent capitalist classes in dependent colonised countries who fight for their 'independence' only on the basis that they will have a share of the pie, a share they conceive of as having its own national identity, that of where they happen to be born.

While the working class is, in its universal

existence, a crucial potential agent in the re-taking of the commons – the commons on a broader higher international level than the local commons enclosed as capitalism took root in different countries – it is also divided. One local working-class is set against the others, and in imperialist countries it can be bought off from time to time, absorbing racist ideas from its own ruling class and functioning as a kind of labour aristocracy in an international quasi-feudal division of labour.

Even so, there is a contradiction at an international level and at a local level in the class struggle against capitalism, and all the more so in times of massive migration; racism that obviously divides workers is countered by practical trade union and political work with asylum-seekers and refugees. Internationalism is not only solidarity with others who are out there in faraway places, but also solidarity through intersectional work across communities in each local context.

Identity

An 'intersectional' approach to the commons and communism is not a combination of different kinds of identity, but throws identity as such into question, whether that is national identity or gender identity or sexual identity. In fact, while intersectional approaches arose first in connecting class, race and gender – from a legal case in which Black women workers were having to confront a legal process that divided them into their different 'identities' in order to weaken their claim – there has been a profound questioning of identity that cuts across these categories from within 'queer' politics.

We can take this further now, and say that we always need to 'queer' identity of any kind in our political struggle at the very same moment as we might tactically lay claim to an identity to build a particular movement. And, to take this further in relation to open communism – the seizing back of the commons so that we may all be free to determine together how to enjoy the fruits of the earth and our own creative labour – we could say that the queering of identity is at the deepest core of internationalism.

Capitalism is good at incorporating radical movements, including lesbian and gay and even trans movements, turning them into consumer market niches, into 'identities' as commodities to be bought and sold. But when there is a queering of identity, a refusal of binary categories of male and female, a questioning of how we are assigned a place in the social order or in the family, capitalism is put under more pressure.

We see this progressive dialectical movement forward in the way that each radical gender and sexual movement takes on a queer aspect when it links with others across community boundaries and national borders; when it, as of necessity, becomes international. Then it opens the way to refusing private property or identity as the property of an individual; it opens the way to communism.

Internationalism enables us to build on our history of struggle for a better world, for a world we have in common, and it does this both by understanding and building on our history, of colonialism and anti-colonial struggle and by understanding and building on our 'identities' and the struggle to remake who we are in order to remake the world.

So, there are two dimensions of struggle at work here in the building of open communism. The first dimension is historical; we learn from the past so that we will not repeat it, and that also means taking care not to romanticise pre-capitalist societies or indigenous peoples as survivals of 'primitive communism' that we simply return to or emulate. We start from where we are, in a world that has been colonised, rendered subject to capital accumulation, globalised, and work together in movements of solidarity, internationalising our common struggle, building working class power, the power of the working class as the universal class.

The second dimension is geographical; we learn from other experiences of struggle so we can better understand how we have been made to live out different national or gendered or sexual identities. We learn the limitations of those identities so we know better how to make claims against capitalism for what is ours, not so we can divide the spoils but so we can share what is rightfully ours. For that we have to internationalise our politics.

10

Plurality

Open communism unites the human race through the working class as the historically-constituted universal class; men and women and those who are non-binary, and those of every apparently separate 'race', work. All who labour, whatever particular 'identity' they choose to describe themselves or feel as they resist oppression, are part of the working class. Many are excluded, 'disabled', but it is a very small proportion of the global population who never work because they are able to choose not to.

There are, we know well, traditions of 'communism' that are closed and bureaucratic, with top-down centralised decision-making apparatuses, but there are many traditions of more plural open communism that connect economic struggle with cultural struggle. The tradition of work on 'hegemony' – the ideological domination of society that serves the ruling class – developed around the 'prison writings' of one of the Italian communist party leaders, is a powerful case example.

The battle of ideas in the struggle for hegemony inside social movements is crucial as a part of the cultural-political work we engage in alongside and inside apparently purely 'economic' struggles. But we need to know what kinds of hegemony count for us as communists and what misreadings of it hold us back.

That tradition also provides an opportunity to clarify what we mean by an intersectional, plural movement of open communism from a revolutionary Marxist standpoint. For there is a dominant reading of arguments about hegemony that led many 'communists' in the so-called 'Eurocommunist' critique of Stalinism to the right; that is, they not only opposed the old closed communism of the bureaucratic states formed after the October revolution in Russia and then in China, but directed attention to an ideological struggle for hegemony that would involve everyone from every class in society.

That kind of 'plurality' is generous and open to a fault, the fault being that class struggle and the strengthening of the working class in all its diversity is replaced with mere liberal plural debate that is hostile to conflict, tries to avoid it, prevent it. Class power and conflict under capitalism, the division between those who own and control the means of production, on the one hand, and those who are exploited – the working class – on the other, is thereby obscured, shut out.

The ideological struggle for 'hegemony' was, in its earliest most useful formulations, in contrast, something that should be occurring inside the working class organisations and exist to strengthen the working class, not weaken it vis-à-vis the ruling class. It is that working-class plurality that lays the basis of open communism.

Standpoint

We can deepen these insights into the importance of a plural open democratic battle of ideas inside the working class – the struggle for hegemony as we work out the best way forward – by including in the working class many standpoints from different kinds of work, different kinds of labour.

From socialist feminism, one of the forms of struggle that revolutionary Marxism now intersects with, come arguments about the position of the exploited and oppressed and what that position allows them to see about power that those with power conveniently place outside of their awareness. That is, awareness and conscious resistance is tied to 'standpoint', and we must learn from the standpoints of those subjected to power if we are to open communism.

Marxism has always been a 'standpoint' theory. It is a theory that is geared to changing what it analyses – the very process of understanding capitalism is linked to practical political activity to resist it – and that is from the standpoint of the working class. Socialist feminism reminds us of that while also reminding us that the position of the women in the family and then as part of the work-force is another specific standpoint as women notice and challenge male power, the rule of men over women, patriarchy.

Women's labour under capitalism is concerned not only with producing things – commodities exchanged for money, a source of profit – but also with maintaining and reproducing the work-force. That is, alongside production is 'social reproduction', and so women who are positioned as caregivers in the field of maternal labour, for example, have a standpoint within the working class that makes their ideological and political contribution different and vital.

Struggles against colonialism and racism deepened this analysis as other standpoints of the oppressed and claims to identity were fought for. Those struggles changed the world, and changed the left. Let's have more of them to re-energise anti-capitalist politics open to communism now.

Ideology

Ideology – the ideas of the ruling class that structure how we all think about the world in line with a certain set of material interests that are not ours – is not a fixed thing, but we can see from all the different cultural productions under capitalism today that it is flexible, mutating to try and incorporate and neutralise threats to it. So, our consciousness of exploitation and oppression also needs to be flexible, tactical about such things as identity, and plural, open to different standpoints.

The same principle applies to the international division of labour historically structured by colonialism and racism. Our internationalism is built into our politics as solidarity with those who are up against imperialism or up against the capitalist state wherever they are, and that means that we notice how different forms of labour produce different standpoints. International working-class organisations, whether as solidarity networks or trade unions or as political groupings, cannot be centralised as if they were a 'world party' governed by the selfsame set of principles applicable to everyone everywhere.

To say that the working class is the 'universal' class is not at all to say that it provides a complete, closed, total or 'totalising' image of what the world is or should be. Universality here means internationalising, and intersectionally so; learning from difference rather than trying to absorb those who are different with the aim of making them the same. We want a movement towards communism in which the future is open.

Argument and debate is at the heart of open communism, and whatever future society we build will be composed of contradictions and antagonisms that structure the debates we have about how to manage our lives, what our relationship is with the fragile ecology of the earth we live on. Communism is not the ending of contradiction, but an ability to work with it instead of trying to snuff it out.

In that sense, all of the hopes of the 'liberals' – that the world should be open to different viewpoints – are only realisable within the communist movement and under communism. Liberals pretend that everyone has an equal say now, that we can jettison the old divisive stuff about class struggle and have a big debate across the social classes, those who are exploited and those who exploit us. This is the road that the liberal 'Eurocommunist' misreading of the battle for 'hegemony' took us in, away from class struggle and to liberal acceptance of the rules of the game that capitalism plays by, so that it always wins, always survives and expands.

Open communism is a society in which class division is abolished, and those who labour share the fruits of their labours so that they are able to manage things so they work less and play more, a society in which liberalism is made possible. You cannot be a liberal apologist for capitalism now if you want that kind of world. You must be anticapitalist, a communist.

11

Transitions

How we open communism, how we get there, is the key question. In fact, that is even more important than dreaming up detailed blueprints for what a communist society will look like. There are many false paths, some of which have led to disaster.

There is a very slow road, cautious and careful not to upset those in power who are determined to protect the private property of the super-rich and corporations to which they are tied through the state apparatus and by a million threads. Here are the social democrats, those who run some of the large electorally-strong 'left' parties, for example, who will bit-by-bit take things so slow the ruling class will not notice. But they will notice, and when the crunch comes the social democrats hesitate, compromise and lead us either back to where we started or into the hands of a brutal military coup they are unprepared to resist.

There is a very fast road, impatient with compromise, quick to denounce anyone building an alliance of the left that will give people confidence and power to demand more. Here are the ultra-left, those who are take up a radical posture that does not really frighten anyone but drives people away from politics because it drives people away from those kinds of sect-like politics. The ruling class can tolerate this quasi-revolutionary play-acting, and just as quickly mobilise people to marginalise and isolate the small groups intent on keeping themselves pure.

Then there is the bureaucratically-organised road-map of the Stalinists who tell us that all human history is neatly-organised into stages and states of development. Here is the comforting romantic story of 'primitive communism' at the beginning of history and then the bad news; the story is that society has to proceed through slavery and then feudalism and then capitalism and then state-organised 'socialism' before arriving at the final goal. The ruling class loves this, for this road takes us through all kinds of delay and pain to justify a long march that is not an appealing alternative to capitalism.

Prefigurative

It was socialist-feminism that reminded us of a transitional strategy that combined an ethical opening of communism now, one that linked social change with personal change. Our future society, the socialist-feminists argued, needs to be anticipated in our forms of struggle. How we organise ourselves now will 'prefigure', and have consequences for the kind of society we are trying to build. This 'prefigurative' politics is transitional, focused on what we need to do now to make the transition to communism.

This brings us up against the limits of the social-democratic strategy that makes us adapt, compromise, and ends up telling us to behave, so then we just reproduce capitalist society as it is now. It brings us up against the manic macho sects that replicate in miniature forms of power that they claim to be against. And it brings us up against the Stalinist tradition that tells us to subordinate our hopes to the existing states and parties that pretend to be 'progressive' or 'socialist', bad mirror-images of capitalist society.

If we really want a society in which there is democratic collective debate about the way forward we need to 'prefigure' that now. Only that will give people the confidence to demand the earth and inspire them to believe that it is worth struggling for.

Means

Just as Marxist analysis of society is intimately linked to transforming its object of study – for it is a revolutionary transformative science of social and personal change – so transitional strategies dialectically link the means of change to its ends. Capitalism is built on hypocrisy, selling us things that promise to make us happy while treating people like objects, turning their labour and their bodies into commodities. Our politics cuts through this hypocrisy, and our vision of communism is profoundly ethical.

Socialist-feminist prefigurative politics returns us to the revolutionary Marxist anti-Stalinist history of a 'transitional' programme for change. Transitional demands include that there be no secret diplomacy, that the books of the companies be opened, and that we directly link wages to inflation so we don't pay for the recurring economic crises that characterise capitalism. Notice that these demands link what is humanly possible now with the kind of society that will be more democratic and just.

These means – a strategy composed of transitional demands and self-organisation of the working class – are what we wish for as the ends we hope to arrive at. An ethical vision of open communism is thus put into practice now so that people experience in their everyday life and political struggle what they are aiming for. This is instead of hypocritically and unethically manipulating people in the vain hope that the ends will justify the means.

We are open about our politics, saying what we mean, being clear, for example, that those who opt for reforms instead of revolution are taking a false path. But instead of just denouncing them we engage them in debate, and we may even vote for them to put them to the test, knowing that whatever increases people's confidence and power will enable people to insist that what they have asked for is reasonable and fair.

For that, alliances and united front organisation with those we disagree with will be necessary to build a context in which we can better build independent working-class self-organisation through the unions and progressive social movements.

Capitalism saps our strength and is already, for most people in the world, a form of barbarism. So to argue – as the revolutionary Marxist Rosa Luxemburg did – that the choice we face now is 'socialism or barbarism' is not between far-off future options. The choice is between the barbarism that capitalism is now and a genuinely socialist alternative that we can build now in the process of building anti-capitalist resistance, open communism.

FURTHER READING

For more analyses of what has gone wrong on the left and resources to put it right again in collective democratic revolutionary struggle, these six books are a good start:

Fisher, M. (2009) *Capitalist Realism: Is there no alternative?* Washington and Winchester: Zero Books. [This book sets the scene for the world we live in now, one in which every possibility for change seems bought off and we are rendered powerless with consumption of commodities being our only escape, but the analysis opens possibilities for moving beyond capitalism]

Mandel, E. (2020) *Introduction to Marxist Theory, Selected Writings.* London: Resistance Books. [This collection of writings by a leading Trotskyist theoretician of the Fourth International shows a different, resolutely non-Stalinist way of thinking about the state, imperialism, bureaucracy and revolutionary organisation]

Parker, I. (2020) *Socialisms: Revolutions Betrayed, Mislaid and Unmade*. London: Resistance Books. [Part travelogue and part analysis, this series of essays gives an account of revolutions and their outcome in Russia, Georgia, Serbia, North Korea, China, Cuba, Laos and Venezuela]

Rowbotham, S., Segal, L. and Wainwright, H. (2013) *Beyond the Fragments: Feminism and the Making of Socialism (3rd Edition)*. Pontypool Wales: Merlin. [This brings together three socialist feminist analyses of encounters with revolutionary organisation in three different non-Stalinist traditions, reflecting on pitfalls and opportunities to do something different]

Samary, C. and Leplat, F. (eds) (2020) *Decolonial Communism, Democracy and the Commons*. London: Resistance Books. [This book brings together a series of anti-Stalinist essays on the intimate links between revolution and colonialism, with attention to ecosocialist politics and critique of actually-existing socialist states]

Trotsky, L. (1937) *The Revolution Betrayed: What is the Soviet Union and Where is it Going?* Online at https://www.marxists.org/archive/trotsky/1936/revbet/index.htm [This classic text was written in exile by one of the leaders of the Russian Revolution who resisted the rise of the Stalinist bureaucracy and who was part of a 'left opposition' that tried to keep alive the spirit of October]

You probably know what these terms mean, or get the idea from reading the book, but here is how we understand these terms. **Anarchism** is a political tradition very suspicious of bureaucracy, and we learn a lot from it while insisting that organisation is necessary to combat the organised capitalist state. **Belt-and-road** is a communication infrastructure run from Beijing to increase the global reach of the regime and make poor countries dependent in the name of development. **Capitalism** is a political-economic system based on exploitation and class privilege that became dominant in the world in the nineteenth and twentieth centuries. **Democratic centralism** is an attempt to collectivise experience, good, and impose order in left organisations, bad, that is too-often more 'centralised' than it is democratic. **Dialectics** is an analytic strategy that emphasises the role of internal contradictions and possibilities of change inside societies and social movements. **Ecosocialism** grounds left and feminist politics in our relation to the natural world, organising against capitalism that prioritises profit and is destroying the planet. **Eurocommunism** was a movement that was neither 'Euro' nor communist in the 1970s inside different communist parties wanting to distance themselves from the Soviet Union. **Hegemony** was described by Italian communist Antonio Gramsci as ideological and cultural leadership in the working-class movement, something we need to actively engage in. **Intersectionality** seeks ways of combining the experiences of the oppressed while respecting the different forms of exploitation and abuse that impact on people and politicise them. **LGBTQI+** political movements organise around lesbian, gay, bisexual, transgender, queer, intersex and other experiences of gender and sexual oppression. **Maoism** is a form of Stalinism, named after Mao Zedong, who broke from Stalin to lead the Chinese revolution and then ruled a bureaucratic regime and a network of left groups to support it. **Patriarchy** is a system of rule, structural inside families and ideological in demeaning and patronising images of women, by men over women and older men over younger men. **Pinkwashing** is the cynical use of lesbian and gay-friendly ideas to cover over actual abuses of power and give legitimacy to regimes that actually care nothing about sexual oppression. **Realism** is an approach that claims to know what things really exist and count, useful in scientific research but problematic when used to close down debate in politics. **Stalinism** is the ideology and practice of the bureaucracy that crystallised around Joseph Stalin in the Soviet Union and replicated itself in communist parties around the world.

Anti*Capitalist Resistance is an organisation of revolutionary socialists. We believe red-green revolution is necessary to meet the compound crisis of humanity and the planet.

We are internationalists, ecosocialists, and anti-capitalist revolutionaries. We oppose imperialism, nationalism, and militarism, and all forms of discrimination, oppression, and bigotry. We support the self-organisation of women, Black people, disabled people, and LGBTQI+ people. We support all oppressed people fighting imperialism and forms of apartheid, and struggling for self-determination, including the people of Palestine.

We favour mass resistance to neoliberal capitalism. We work inside existing mass organisations, but we believe grassroots struggle to be the core of effective resistance, and that the emancipation of the working class and the oppressed will be the act of the working class and the oppressed ourselves.

We reject forms of left organisation that focus exclusively on electoralism and social-democratic reforms. We also oppose top-down 'democratic-centralist' models. We favour a pluralist organization that can learn from struggles at home and across the world.

We aim to build a united organisation, rooted in the struggles of the working class and the oppressed, and committed to debate, initiative, and self-activity. We are for social transformation, based on mass participatory democracy.

info@anticapitalistresistance.org
www.anticapitalistresistance.org

ABOUT RESISTANCE BOOKS

Resistance Books is a radical publisher of internationalist, ecosocialist, and feminist books. We publish books in collaboration with the International Institute for Research and Education in Amsterdam (www.iire.org) and the Fourth International (www.fourth.international/en). For further information, including a full list of titles available and how to order them, go to the Resistance Books website.

info@resistancebooks.org
www.resistancebooks.org